Life Lessons

from THE INSPIRED WORD of GOD

BOOK of GENESIS

MAX LUCADO

General Editor

D1166276

LIFE LESSONS FROM THE INSPIRED WORD OF GOD—BOOK OF GENESIS
Copyright © 1997, Word Publishing. All rights reserved. No portion of this book may be reproduced, stored in a retrieval system, or transmitted in any form or by any means—electronic, mechanical, photocopy, recording, or any other—except for brief quotations in printed reviews, without the prior permission of the publisher.

Scripture passages taken from:

 The Holy Bible, *New Century Version*
Copyright ©1987, 1988, 1991 by Word Publishing. All rights reserved.

 The Holy Bible, *New King James Version*
Copyright © 1979, 1980, 1982 by Thomas Nelson. All rights reserved.

All excerpts used by permission.

Design and cover art—by Koechel Peterson and Associates, Inc., Minneapolis, Minnesota.

Produced with the assistance of the Livingstone Corporation.

ISBN: 0-8499-5320-0
Published by Word Publishing

All rights reserved. *Printed in the United States of America.*

TABLE OF CONTENTS

HOW TO STUDY THE BIBLE

BY MAX LUCADO

*T*his is a peculiar book you are holding. Words crafted in another language. Deeds done in a distant era. Events recorded in a far-off land. Counsel offered to a foreign people. This is a peculiar book.

It's surprising that anyone reads it. It's too old. Some of its writings date back five thousand years. It's too bizarre. The book speaks of incredible floods, fires, earthquakes, and people with supernatural abilities. It's too radical. The Bible calls for undying devotion to a carpenter who called himself God's Son.

Logic says this book shouldn't survive. Too old, too bizarre, too radical.

The Bible has been banned, burned, scoffed, and ridiculed. Scholars have mocked it as foolish. Kings have branded it as illegal. A thousand times over it the grave has been dug and the dirge has begun, but somehow the Bible never stays in the grave. Not only has it survived, it has thrived. It is the single most popular book in all of history. It has been the best-selling book in the world for years!

There is no way on earth to explain it. Which perhaps is the only explanation. The answer? The Bible's durability is not found on earth; it is found in heaven. For the millions who have tested its claims and claimed its promises, there is but one answer—the Bible is God's book and God's voice.

As you read it, you would be wise to give some thought to two questions. What is the purpose of the Bible? and How do I study the Bible? Time spent reflecting on these two issues will greatly enhance your Bible study.

What is the purpose of the Bible?

Let the Bible itself answer that question.

Since you were a child you have known the Holy Scriptures which are able to make you wise. And that wisdom leads to salvation through faith in Christ Jesus.

(2 Tim. 3:15)

The purpose of the Bible? Salvation. God's highest passion is to get his children home. His book, the Bible, describes his plan of salvation. The purpose of the Bible is to proclaim God's plan and passion to save his children.

That is the reason this book has endured through the centuries. It dares to tackle the toughest questions about life: Where do I go after I die? Is there a God? What do I do with my fears? The Bible offers answers to these crucial questions. It is the treasure map that leads us to God's highest treasure, eternal life.

But how do we use the Bible? Countless copies of Scripture sit unread on bookshelves and nightstands simply because people don't know how to read it. What can we do to make the Bible real in our lives?

The clearest answer is found in the words of Jesus.

"Ask," he promised, *"and God will give it to you. Search and you will find. Knock, and the door will open for you."*

(Matt. 7:7)

The first step in understanding the Bible is asking God to help us. We should read prayerfully. If anyone understands God's Word, it is because of God and not the reader.

But the Helper will teach you everything and will cause you to remember all that I told you. The Helper is the Holy Spirit whom the Father will send in my name.

(John 14:24)

Before reading the Bible, pray. Invite God to speak to you. Don't go to Scripture looking for your idea, go searching for his.

Not only should we read the Bible prayerfully, we should read it carefully. *Search and you will find* is the pledge. The Bible is not a newspaper to be skimmed but rather a mine to be quarried. *Search for it like silver, and hunt for it like hidden treasure. Then you will understand respect for the LORD, and you will find that you know God* (Prov. 2:4).

Any worthy find requires effort. The Bible is no exception. To understand the Bible you don't have to be brilliant, but you must be willing to roll up your sleeves and search.

Be a worker who is not ashamed and who uses the true teaching in the right way.

(2 Tim. 2:15)

Here's a practical point. Study the Bible a bit at a time. Hunger is not satisfied by eating twenty-one meals in one sitting once a week. The body needs a steady diet to remain strong. So does the soul. When God sent food to his people in the wilderness, he didn't provide loaves already made. Instead, he sent them manna in the shape of *thin flakes, like frost . . . on the desert ground* (Exod. 16:14).

God gave manna in limited portions.

God sends spiritual food the same way. He opens the heavens with just enough nutrients for today's hunger. He provides, *a command here, a command there. A rule here, a rule there. A little lesson here, a little lesson there* (Isa. 28:10).

Don't be discouraged if your reading reaps a small harvest. Some days a lesser portion is all that is needed. What is important is to search every day for that day's message. A steady diet of God's Word over a lifetime builds a healthy soul and mind.

A little girl returned from her first day at school. Her mom asked, "Did you learn anything?" "Apparently not enough," the girl responded, "I have to go back tomorrow and the next day and the next. . . ."

Such is the case with learning. And such is the case with Bible study. Understanding comes little by little over a lifetime.

There is a third step in understanding the Bible. After the asking and seeking comes the knocking. After you ask and search, then knock.

Knock, and the door will open for you.
(Matt. 7:7)

To knock is to stand at God's door. To make yourself available. To climb the steps, cross the porch, stand at the doorway, and volunteer. Knocking goes beyond the realm of thinking and into the realm of acting.

To knock is to ask, What can I do? How can I obey? Where can I go?

It's one thing to know what to do. It's another to do it. But for those who do it, those who choose to obey, a special reward awaits them.

The truly happy are those who carefully study God's perfect law that makes people free, and they continue to study it. They do not forget what they heard, but they obey what God's teaching says. Those who do this will be made happy.
(James 1:25)

What a promise. Happiness comes to those who do what they read! It's the same with medicine. If you only read the label but ignore the pills, it won't help. It's the same with food. If you only read the recipe but never cook, you won't be fed. And it's the same with the Bible. If you only read the words but never obey, you'll never know the joy God has promised.

Ask. Search. Knock. Simple, isn't it? Why don't you give it a try? If you do, you'll see why you are holding the most remarkable book in history.

GENESIS

INTRODUCTION

So there you are, a teenager at your grandparent's house. You don't really want to be there, but it's one of those family things, and so you're there.

You sit politely and act like you are listening as your folks and grandparents talk. Then your grandmother says something that catches your attention. She refers to your great-grandfather and the trip he made to America from the "old country."

"What?" you ask.

Grandma smiles, knowing that at some point we all wonder about our origin and here you are wondering about yours.

She unravels a tale of your family escaping persecution and settling in eastern Virginia. Next she invites you into her room, where she opens a large chest that has sat at the foot of her bed for as long as you can remember. A rush of cedar and mothballs fills the room.

"Thought you might like to see this," she explains, handing you a black-and-white photo in a large walnut frame. "It's your great-grandpa." The only thing stiffer than his collar is his expression. "Here is his father," she hands you another photo, one of a cowboy wearing a wide-brimmed hat, riding a horse.

Piece by piece, the chest tells its family tales. Soon you find yourself lost in a floor covered with old wedding gowns, photo albums, diplomas, and bronzed baby shoes. And before you leave, you find yourself the owner of something precious—a heritage. An ancestry. A beginning. An origin.

You know that you are a part of a family tree. You aren't an isolated pond, but rather a part of a river winding though a great canyon.

You leave a richer person. Knowing where you came from says much about where you are going.

Perhaps that's why the first book of the Bible is a book of beginnings. God wants us to know from where we came. Learning that will teach us much about the place we are going.

LESSON ONE

CREATION

REFLECTION

Begin your study by sharing thoughts on this idea.

1. Describe a fascinating part of God's creation.

_____

_____

_____

BIBLE READING

Read Genesis 2:4–25 from the NCV or NKJV.

NCV

⁴This is the story of the creation of the sky and the earth. When the LORD God first made the earth and the sky, ⁵there were still no plants on the earth. Nothing was growing in the fields because the LORD God had not yet made it rain on the land. And there was no person to care for the ground, ⁶but a mist would rise up from the earth and water all the ground.

⁷Then the LORD God took dust from the ground and formed a man from it. He breathed the breath of life into the man's nose, and the

NKJV

⁴This _is_ the history of the heavens and the earth when they were created, in the day that the LORD God made the earth and the heavens, ⁵before any plant of the field was in the earth and before any herb of the field had grown. For the LORD God had not caused it to rain on the earth, and _there was_ no man to till the ground; ⁶but a mist went up from the earth and watered the whole face of the ground.

⁷And the LORD God formed man _of_ the dust of the ground, and breathed into his nostrils

NCV

man became a living person. ⁸Then the LORD God planted a garden in the east, in a place called Eden, and put the man he had formed into it. ⁹The LORD God caused every beautiful tree and every tree that was good for food to grow out of the ground. In the middle of the garden, God put the tree that gives life and also the tree that gives the knowledge of good and evil.

¹⁰A river flowed through Eden and watered the garden. From there the river branched out to become four rivers. ¹¹The first river, named Pishon, flows around the whole land of Havilah, where there is gold. ¹²The gold of that land is excellent. Bdellium and onyx are also found there. ¹³The second river, named Gihon, flows around the whole land of Cush. ¹⁴The third river, named Tigris, flows out of Assyria toward the east. The fourth river is the Euphrates.

¹⁵The LORD God put the man in the garden of Eden to care for it and work it. ¹⁶The LORD God commanded him, "You may eat the fruit from any tree in the garden, ¹⁷but you must not eat the fruit from the tree which gives the knowledge of good and evil. If you ever eat fruit from that tree, you will die!"

¹⁸Then the LORD God said, "It is not good for the man to be alone. I will make a helper who is right for him."

¹⁹From the ground God formed every wild animal and every bird in the sky, and he brought them to the man so the man could name them. Whatever the man called each living thing, that became its name. ²⁰The man gave names to all the tame animals, to the birds in the sky, and to all the wild animals. But Adam

NKJV

the breath of life; and man became a living being.

⁸The LORD God planted a garden eastward in Eden, and there He put the man whom He had formed. ⁹And out of the ground the LORD God made every tree grow that is pleasant to the sight and good for food. The tree of life *was* also in the midst of the garden, and the tree of the knowledge of good and evil.

¹⁰Now a river went out of Eden to water the garden, and from there it parted and became four riverheads. ¹¹The name of the first *is* Pishon; it *is* the one which skirts the whole land of Havilah, where *there is* gold. ¹²And the gold of that land *is* good. Bdellium and the onyx stone *are* there. ¹³The name of the second river *is* Gihon; it *is* the one which goes around the whole land of Cush. ¹⁴The name of the third river *is* Hiddekel; it *is* the one which goes toward the east of Assyria. The fourth river *is* the Euphrates.

¹⁵Then the LORD God took the man and put him in the garden of Eden to tend and keep it. ¹⁶And the LORD God commanded the man, saying, "Of every tree of the garden you may freely eat; ¹⁷but of the tree of the knowledge of good and evil you shall not eat, for in the day that you eat of it you shall surely die."

¹⁸And the LORD God said, "*It is* not good that man should be alone; I will make him a helper comparable to him." ¹⁹Out of the ground the LORD God formed every beast of the field and every bird of the air, and brought *them* to Adam to see what he would call them. And whatever Adam called each living creature, that *was* its name. ²⁰So Adam gave names to all cattle, to the

NCV

did not find a helper that was right for him. ²¹So the LORD God caused the man to sleep very deeply, and while he was asleep, God removed one of the man's ribs. Then God closed up the man's skin at the place where he took the rib. ²²The LORD God used the rib from the man to make a woman, and then he brought the woman to the man.

²³And the man said,

"Now, this is someone whose bones came
from my bones,
whose body came from my body.
I will call her 'woman,'
because she was taken out of man."

²⁴So a man will leave his father and mother and be united with his wife, and the two will become one body.

²⁵The man and his wife were naked, but they were not ashamed.

NKJV

birds of the air, and to every beast of the field. But for Adam there was not found a helper comparable to him.

²¹And the LORD God caused a deep sleep to fall on Adam, and he slept; and He took one of his ribs, and closed up the flesh in its place. ²²Then the rib which the LORD God had taken from man He made into a woman, and He brought her to the man.

²³And Adam said:

"This *is* now bone of my bones
And flesh of my flesh;
She shall be called Woman,
Because she was taken out of Man."

²⁴Therefore a man shall leave his father and mother and be joined to his wife, and they shall become one flesh.

²⁵And they were both naked, the man and his wife, and were not ashamed.

DISCOVERY

Explore the Bible reading by discussing these questions.

2. Why did God choose to create the heavens and the earth?

_____

_____

_____

3. In what ways did God make Adam responsible for the earth?

_____

_____

_____

4. What is the significance of Adam coming from the dust of the ground and God breathing life into him?

_____

_____

_____

5. What reasons could God have for making woman from man and not from the earth?

_____

_____

_____

6. Why did God give Adam a choice about the tree rather than physically preventing him from eating the fruit?

_____

_____

_____

INSPIRATION

Here is an uplifting thought from *The Inspirational Bible*.

He placed one scoop of clay upon another until a form lay lifeless on the ground. . . .

All were silent as the Creator reached in himself and removed something yet unseen. "It's called 'choice.' The seed of choice."

Creation stood in silence and gazed upon the lifeless form.

An angel spoke, "But what if he . . ."

"What if he chooses not to love?" the Creator finished. "Come, I will show you."

Unbound by today, God and the angel walked into the realm of tomorrow. . . .

The angel gasped at what he saw. Spontaneous love. Voluntary devotion. Never had he seen anything like these. . . .The angel stood speechless as they passed through centuries of repugnance. Never had he seen such filth. Rotten hearts. Ruptured promises. Forgotten loyalties. . . .

The Creator walked on in time, further and further into the future, until he stood by a tree. A tree that would be fashioned into a cradle. Even then he could smell the hay that would surround him. . . .

"Wouldn't it be easier to not plant the seed? Wouldn't it be easier to not give the choice?"

"It would," the Creator spoke slowly. "But to remove the choice is to remove the love."

. . . They stepped into the Garden again. The Maker looked earnestly at the clay creation.

A monsoon of love swelled up within him. He had died for the creation before he had made him. God's form bent over the sculptured face and breathed. Dust stirred on the lips of the new one. The chest rose, cracking the red mud. The cheeks fleshened. A finger moved. And an eye opened.

But more incredible than the moving of the flesh was the stirring of the spirit. Those who could see the unseen gasped.

Perhaps it was the wind who said it first. Perhaps what the star saw that moment is what has made it blink ever since. Maybe it was left to an angel to whisper it:

"It looks like . . . it appears so much like . . . it is him!"

The angel wasn't speaking of the face, the features, or the body. He was looking inside at the soul.

"It's eternal!" gasped another.

Within the man, God had placed a divine seed. A seed of his self. The God of might had created earth's mightiest. The Creator had created, not a creature, but another creator. And the One who had chosen to love had created one who could love in return.

Now it's our choice.

(From *In the Eye of the Storm*
by Max Lucado)

RESPONSE

Use these questions to share more deeply with each other.

7. Describe how Adam might have felt when he saw Eve for the first time.

_____

_____

_____

8. What can we learn about ourselves from this lesson's Bible passage?

_____

_____

_____

9. What does the creation reveal about God?

_____

_____

_____

PRAYER

Father, we stand in awe of your wonderful handiwork. Your majesty surrounds us. Thank you for providing the opportunity to have a relationship with you, the giver of life and the Creator of all the universe.

JOURNALING

Take a few moments to record your personal insights from this lesson.

How can I express my appreciation to God for his creation?

ADDITIONAL QUESTIONS

10. What must it have been like for Adam to be the only human in the garden?

_____

_____

_____

11. Despite being naked, why did Adam and Eve feel no shame?

_____

_____

_____

12. What does this lesson's Bible passage teach about marriage?

_____

_____

_____

For more Bible passages about God's creation, see Job 32:8; Psalm 19:1; 104:1–35; and Ecclesiastes 12:7.

To complete the Book of Genesis during this twelve-part study, read Genesis 1:1–2:25.

LESSON TWO

SIN AND ITS CONSEQUENCES

REFLECTION

Begin your study by sharing thoughts on this question.

1. Think back to when you were a child. What were the consequences of disobeying your parents?

_____

_____

_____

BIBLE READING

Read Genesis 3:1–23 from the NCV or the NKJV.

NCV

¹Now the snake was the most clever of all the wild animals the LORD God had made. One day the snake said to the woman, "Did God really say that you must not eat fruit from any tree in the garden?"

²The woman answered the snake, "We may eat fruit from the trees in the garden. ³But God told us, 'You must not eat fruit from the tree that is in the middle of the garden. You must not even touch it, or you will die.'"

⁴But the snake said to the woman, "You will

NKJV

¹Now the serpent was more cunning than any beast of the field which the LORD God had made. And he said to the woman, "Has God indeed said, 'You shall not eat of every tree of the garden'?"

²And the woman said to the serpent, "We may eat the fruit of the trees of the garden; ³"but of the fruit of the tree which _is_ in the midst of the garden, God has said, 'You shall not eat it, nor shall you touch it, lest you die.'"

⁴Then the serpent said to the woman, "You

NCV

not die. ⁵God knows that if you eat the fruit from that tree, you will learn about good and evil and you will be like God!"

⁶The woman saw that the tree was beautiful, that its fruit was good to eat, and that it would make her wise. So she took some of its fruit and ate it. She also gave some of the fruit to her husband, and he ate it.

⁷Then, it was as if their eyes were opened. They realized they were naked, so they sewed fig leaves together and made something to cover themselves.

⁸Then they heard the LORD God walking in the garden during the cool part of the day, and the man and his wife hid from the LORD God among the trees in the garden. ⁹But the LORD God called to the man and said, "Where are you?"

¹⁰The man answered, "I heard you walking in the garden, and I was afraid because I was naked, so I hid."

¹¹God asked, "Who told you that you were naked? Did you eat fruit from the tree from which I commanded you not to eat?"

¹²The man said, "You gave this woman to me and she gave me fruit from the tree, so I ate it."

¹³Then the LORD God said to the woman, "How could you have done such a thing?"

She answered, "The snake tricked me, so I ate the fruit."

¹⁴The LORD God said to the snake,

"Because you did this,
　a curse will be put on you.
　　You will be cursed as no other animal,
　　　tame or wild, will ever be.
　You will crawl on your stomach,

NKJV

will not surely die. ⁵For God knows that in the day you eat of it your eyes will be opened, and you will be like God, knowing good and evil."

⁶So when the woman saw that the tree *was* good for food, that it *was* pleasant to the eyes, and a tree desirable to make *one* wise, she took of its fruit and ate. She also gave to her husband with her, and he ate. ⁷Then the eyes of both of them were opened, and they knew that they *were* naked; and they sewed fig leaves together and made themselves coverings.

⁸And they heard the sound of the LORD God walking in the garden in the cool of the day, and Adam and his wife hid themselves from the presence of the LORD God among the trees of the garden.

⁹Then the LORD God called to Adam and said to him, "Where *are* you?"

¹⁰So he said, "I heard Your voice in the garden, and I was afraid because I was naked; and I hid myself."

¹¹And He said, "Who told you that you *were* naked? Have you eaten from the tree of which I commanded you that you should not eat?"

¹²Then the man said, "The woman whom You gave *to be* with me, she gave me of the tree, and I ate."

¹³And the LORD God said to the woman, "What *is* this you have done?"

The woman said, "The serpent deceived me, and I ate."

¹⁴So the LORD God said to the serpent:

"Because you have done this,
　You *are* cursed more than all cattle,
　And more than every beast of the field;

NCV

and you will eat dust all the days of
　　your life.
¹⁵ I will make you and the woman
　　enemies to each other.
Your descendants and her descendants
　　will be enemies.
One of her descendants will crush your
　　head,
　　and you will bite his heel."

¹⁶Then God said to the woman,
"I will cause you to have much trouble
　　when you are pregnant,
and when you give birth to children,
　　you will have great pain.
You will greatly desire your husband,
　　but he will rule over you."

¹⁷Then God said to the man, "You listened to
what your wife said, and you ate fruit from the
tree from which I commanded you not to eat.
"So I will put a curse on the ground,
　　and you will have to work very hard
　　　for your food.
In pain you will eat its food
　　all the days of your life.
¹⁸ The ground will produce thorns and
　　weeds for you,
　　and you will eat the plants of the field.
¹⁹ You will sweat and work hard
　　for your food.
Later you will return to the ground,
　　because you were taken from it.
You are dust,
　　and when you die, you will return to
　　　the dust."

NKJV

On your belly you shall go,
And you shall eat dust
All the days of your life.
¹⁵　And I will put enmity
Between you and the woman,
And between your seed and her Seed;
He shall bruise your head,
And you shall bruise His heel."

¹⁶　To the woman He said:

"I will greatly multiply your sorrow and
　　your conception;
In pain you shall bring forth children;
Your desire *shall be* for your husband,
And he shall rule over you."

¹⁷Then to Adam He said, "Because you have
heeded the voice of your wife, and have eaten
from the tree of which I commanded you, saying, 'You shall not eat of it':

"Cursed *is* the ground for your sake;
In toil you shall eat *of* it
All the days of your life.
¹⁸　Both thorns and thistles it shall bring forth
　　for you,
And you shall eat the herb of the field.
¹⁹　In the sweat of your face you shall eat bread
Till you return to the ground,
For out of it you were taken;
For dust you *are,*
And to dust you shall return."

²⁰And Adam called his wife's name Eve,
because she was the mother of all living.

NCV

²⁰The man named his wife Eve, because she is the mother of everyone who has ever lived.

²¹The LORD God made clothes from animal skins for the man and his wife and dressed them. ²²Then the LORD God said, "The man has become like one of us; he knows good and evil. We must keep him from eating some of the fruit from the tree of life, or he will live forever." ²³So the LORD God forced the man out of the garden of Eden to work the ground from which he was taken.

NKJV

²¹Also for Adam and his wife the LORD God made tunics of skin, and clothed them.

²²Then the LORD God said, "Behold, the man has become like one of Us, to know good and evil. And now, lest he put out his hand and take also of the tree of life, and eat, and live forever"— ²³therefore the LORD God sent him out of the garden of Eden to till the ground from which he was taken.

DISCOVERY

Explore the Bible reading by discussing these questions.

2. Why did Eve choose to eat the fruit?

_____

_____

_____

3. Why was shame one of the most immediate results of the sin of Adam and Eve?

_____

_____

_____

4. What consequences did Adam and Eve experience that we still experience today when we sin?

_____

_____

_____

5. Words like "openness" and "community" described the relationship of God with Adam and Eve before sin. What words describe their relationship afterward?

_____

_____

_____

6. How did Adam's sin affect his relationship with God?

_____

_____

_____

INSPIRATION

Here is an uplifting thought from *The Inspirational Bible.*

Real change is an inside job. You might alter things a day or two with money and systems, but the heart of the matter is, and always will be, the matter of the heart.

Allow me to get specific. Our problem is sin. Not finances. Not budgets. Not overcrowded prisons or drug dealers. Our problem is sin. We are in rebellion against our Creator. We are separated from our Father. We are cut off from the source of life. A new president or policy won't fix that. It can only be solved by God.

That's why the Bible uses drastic terms like *conversion, repentance,* and *lost* and *found.* Society may renovate, but only God re-creates.

Here is a practical exercise to put this truth into practice. The next time alarms go off in your world, ask yourself three questions.

1. Is there any unconfessed sin in my life? . . .
2. Are there any unresolved conflicts in my world? . . .
3. Are there any unsurrendered worries in my heart? . . .

Alarms serve a purpose. They signal a problem. Sometimes the problem is out there. More often it's in here. So before you peek outside, take a good look inside.

(From *When God Whispers Your Name* by Max Lucado)

RESPONSE

Use these questions to share more deeply with each other.

7. What happens to our relationship with God when we sin?

_____

_____

_____

8. In what ways does sin affect our relationship with others?

_____

_____

_____

9. Even though we know the consequences of sin, why do we sometimes still choose to disobey?

_____

_____

_____

PRAYER

Father, too often we flirt with temptation and rationalize our actions only to find ourselves far from you. Help us to learn from the consequences of our sin, and bring us back into a right relationship with you.

JOURNALING

Take a few moments to record your personal insights from this lesson.

What have I learned from the consequences of my past sins?

ADDITIONAL QUESTIONS

10. Why would God plant a tree in the garden and then forbid Adam and Eve to eat from it?

_____

_____

_____

11. In what ways has Adam and Eve's sin affected all humanity?

_____

_____

_____

12. What is God's plan to defeat Satan and sin?

_____

_____

_____

For more Bible passages about sin and its consequences, see 1 Chronicles 13; Nehemiah 9; Proverbs 19:16; Hosea 4:1–10; Romans 5:12–20; James 1:12–15.

To complete the Book of Genesis during this twelve-part study, read Genesis 3:1–5:32.

ADDITIONAL THOUGHTS

LESSON THREE

OBEDIENCE TO GOD

REFLECTION

Begin your study by sharing thoughts on this question.

1. Think of a time when you were asked to do something that seemed ridiculous. Why did you do it?

_____

_____

_____

BIBLE READING

Read Genesis 7:1–16 from the NCV or NKJV.

NCV

¹Then the LORD said to Noah, "I have seen that you are the best person among the people of this time, so you and your family can go into the boat. ²Take with you seven pairs, each male with its female, of every kind of clean animal, and take one pair, each male with its female, of every kind of unclean animal. ³Take seven pairs of all the birds of the sky, each male with its female. This will allow all these animals to continue living on the earth after the flood. ⁴Seven days from now I will send rain on the

NKJV

¹Then the LORD said to Noah, "Come into the ark, you and all your household, because I have seen *that* you *are* righteous before Me in this generation. ²You shall take with you seven each of every clean animal, a male and his female; two each of animals that *are* unclean, a male and his female; ³also seven each of birds of the air, male and female, to keep the species alive on the face of all the earth. ⁴For after seven more days I will cause it to rain on the earth forty days and forty nights, and I will destroy

NCV

earth. It will rain forty days and forty nights, and I will wipe off from the earth every living thing that I have made."

⁵Noah did everything the LORD commanded him.

⁶Noah was six hundred years old when the flood came. ⁷He and his wife and his sons and their wives went into the boat to escape the waters of the flood. ⁸The clean animals, the unclean animals, the birds, and everything that crawls on the ground ⁹came to Noah. They went into the boat in groups of two, male and female, just as God had commanded Noah. ¹⁰Seven days later the flood started.

¹¹When Noah was six hundred years old, the flood started. On the seventeenth day of the second month of that year the underground springs split open, and the clouds in the sky poured out rain. ¹²The rain fell on the earth for forty days and forty nights.

¹³On that same day Noah and his wife, his sons Shem, Ham, and Japheth, and their wives went into the boat. ¹⁴They had every kind of wild and tame animal, every kind of animal that crawls on the earth, and every kind of bird. ¹⁵Every creature that had the breath of life came to Noah in the boat in groups of two. ¹⁶One male and one female of every living thing came, just as God had commanded Noah. Then the LORD closed the door behind them.

NKJV

from the face of the earth all living things that I have made." ⁵And Noah did according to all that the LORD commanded him. ⁶Noah *was* six hundred years old when the floodwaters were on the earth.

⁷So Noah, with his sons, his wife, and his sons' wives, went into the ark because of the waters of the flood. ⁸Of clean animals, of animals that *are* unclean, of birds, and of everything that creeps on the earth, ⁹two by two they went into the ark to Noah, male and female, as God had commanded Noah. ¹⁰And it came to pass after seven days that the waters of the flood were on the earth. ¹¹In the six hundredth year of Noah's life, in the second month, the seventeenth day of the month, on that day all the fountains of the great deep were broken up, and the windows of heaven were opened. ¹²And the rain was on the earth forty days and forty nights.

¹³On the very same day Noah and Noah's sons, Shem, Ham, and Japheth, and Noah's wife and the three wives of his sons with them, entered the ark— ¹⁴they and every beast after its kind, all cattle after their kind, every creeping thing that creeps on the earth after its kind, and every bird after its kind, every bird of every sort. ¹⁵And they went into the ark to Noah, two by two, of all flesh in which *is* the breath of life. ¹⁶So those that entered, male and female of all flesh, went in as God had commanded him; and the LORD shut him in.

DISCOVERY

Explore the Bible reading by discussing these questions.

2. What do you think Noah was thinking when God asked him to collect the animals and enter the ark?

_____

_____

_____

3. What issues did Noah face in doing what God instructed that we face today?

_____

_____

_____

4. What words or phrases describe how Noah responded to God's instructions?

_____

_____

_____

5. Noah obeyed God without question in regards to building an ark. What does that say about how he obeyed God in everyday, little things?

_____

_____

_____

6. What does this lesson's Bible passage reveal about Noah's character?

_____

_____

_____

INSPIRATION

Here is an uplifting thought from *The Inspirational Bible.*

I have found that the casual Christian has little or no influence upon others. I am finding that it is only the Christian who refuses to compromise in matters of honesty, integrity, and morality who is bearing an effective witness for Christ. The worldly Christian is prepared to do as the world does and will condone practices which are dishonest and unethical because he is afraid of the world's displeasure. Only by a life of obedience to the voice of the Spirit, by daily dying to self, by a full dedication to Christ and constant fellowship with Him, are we able to live a godly life and have a positive influence in this present ungodly world.

(From *Unto the Hills*
by Billy Graham)

RESPONSE

Use these questions to share more deeply with each other.

7. Imagine yourself in Noah's situation. How would you have responded to God?

_____

_____

_____

8. In what ways does obedience to God often require a step of faith?

_____

_____

_____

9. Why is it sometimes difficult to obey God's commands?

_____

_____

_____

PRAYER

Sometimes, Father, you ask us to do things that we don't understand. We question, hesitate, and struggle to obey. Draw us closer to you so we will have the confidence to take that step of faith and do as you ask.

JOURNALING

Take a few moments to record your personal insights from this lesson.

In what ways do I struggle with obeying God?

ADDITIONAL QUESTIONS

10. In what ways has God rewarded your obedience to him?

_____

_____

_____

11. How can your obedience to God have an influence on others?

_____

_____

_____

12. What attitudes are typical of people whose obedience to God you greatly respect?

_____

_____

_____

For more Bible passages about obedience, see Deuteronomy 4:1-14; Psalm 37; 128; Proverbs 19:23; Daniel 1; 3; Matthew 1:18–25; Acts 26.

To complete the Book of Genesis during this twelve-part study, read Genesis 6:1–10:32.

ADDITIONAL THOUGHTS

LESSON FOUR

GOD'S PROMISES

REFLECTION

Begin your study by sharing thoughts on this question.

1. Think back to an important promise you made. In what ways were you faithful to that promise?

_____

_____

_____

BIBLE READING

Read Genesis 15:1–18 from the NCV or NKJV.

NCV

¹After these things happened, the LORD spoke his word to Abram in a vision: "Abram, don't be afraid. I will defend you, and I will give you a great reward."

²But Abram said, "Lord GOD, what can you give me? I have no son, so my slave Eliezer from Damascus will get everything I own after I die." ³Abram said, "Look, you have given me no son, so a slave born in my house will inherit everything I have."

⁴Then the LORD spoke his word to Abram:

NKJV

¹After these things the word of the LORD came to Abram in a vision, saying, "Do not be afraid, Abram. I *am* your shield, your exceedingly great reward."

²But Abram said, "Lord GOD, what will You give me, seeing I go childless, and the heir of my house *is* Eliezer of Damascus?" ³Then Abram said, "Look, You have given me no offspring; indeed one born in my house is my heir!"

⁴And behold, the word of the LORD *came* to

NCV

"He will not be the one to inherit what you have. You will have a son of your own who will inherit what you have."

⁵Then God led Abram outside and said, "Look at the sky. There are so many stars you cannot count them. Your descendants also will be too many to count."

⁶Abram believed the LORD. And the LORD accepted Abram's faith, and that faith made him right with God.

⁷God said to Abram, "I am the LORD who led you out of Ur of Babylonia so that I could give you this land to own."

⁸But Abram said, "Lord GOD, how can I be sure that I will own this land?"

⁹The LORD said to Abram, "Bring me a three-year-old cow, a three-year-old goat, a three-year-old male sheep, a dove, and a young pigeon."

¹⁰Abram brought them all to God. Then Abram killed the animals and cut each of them into two pieces, laying each half opposite the other half. But he did not cut the birds in half. ¹¹Later, large birds flew down to eat the animals, but Abram chased them away.

¹²As the sun was going down, Abram fell into a deep sleep. While he was asleep, a very terrible darkness came. ¹³Then the LORD said to Abram, "You can be sure that your descendants will be strangers and travel in a land they don't own. The people there will make them slaves and be cruel to them for four hundred years. ¹⁴But I will punish the nation where they are slaves. Then your descendants will leave that land, taking great wealth with them. ¹⁵And you, Abram, will die in peace and will be

NKJV

him, saying, "This one shall not be your heir, but one who will come from your own body shall be your heir." ⁵Then He brought him outside and said, "Look now toward heaven, and count the stars if you are able to number them." And He said to him, "So shall your descendants be."

⁶And he believed in the LORD, and He accounted it to him for righteousness.

⁷Then He said to him, "I *am* the LORD, who brought you out of Ur of the Chaldeans, to give you this land to inherit it."

⁸And he said, "Lord GOD, how shall I know that I will inherit it?"

⁹So He said to him, "Bring Me a three-year-old heifer, a three-year-old female goat, a three-year-old ram, a turtledove, and a young pigeon." ¹⁰Then he brought all these to Him and cut them in two, down the middle, and placed each piece opposite the other; but he did not cut the birds in two. ¹¹And when the vultures came down on the carcasses, Abram drove them away.

¹²Now when the sun was going down, a deep sleep fell upon Abram; and behold, horror *and* great darkness fell upon him. ¹³Then He said to Abram: "Know certainly that your descendants will be strangers in a land *that is* not theirs, and will serve them, and they will afflict them four hundred years. ¹⁴"And also the nation whom they serve I will judge; afterward they shall come out with great possessions. ¹⁵"Now as for you, you shall go to your fathers in peace; you shall be buried at a good old age. ¹⁶"But in the fourth generation they shall return here, for the iniquity of the Amorites *is* not yet complete."

NCV

buried at an old age. ¹⁶After your great-great-grandchildren are born, your people will come to this land again. It will take that long, because I am not yet going to punish the Amorites for their evil behavior."

¹⁷After the sun went down, it was very dark. Suddenly a smoking firepot and a blazing torch passed between the halves of the dead animals. ¹⁸So on that day the LORD made an agreement with Abram and said, "I will give to your descendants the land between the river of Egypt and the great river Euphrates.

NKJV

¹⁷And it came to pass, when the sun went down and it was dark, that behold, there appeared a smoking oven and a burning torch that passed between those pieces. ¹⁸On the same day the LORD made a covenant with Abram, saying: "To your descendants I have given this land, from the river of Egypt to the great river, the River Euphrates—

DISCOVERY

Explore the Bible reading by discussing these questions.

2. What did it mean to Abram that he had no son?

_____

_____

_____

3. God promised Abram that he would inherit the land. Why did Abram have difficulty believing God's promise?

_____

_____

_____

4. God brought supernatural fire to burn Abram's sacrifices. How did this confirm Abram's faith?

_____

_____

_____

5. What do you think might have been Abram's reaction to God's miracle of fire?

_____

_____

_____

6. God credited Abram with righteousness because of his faith. What does that say about our own righteousness?

_____

_____

_____

INSPIRATION

Here is an uplifting thought from *The Inspirational Bible.*

Abraham, or Abram as he was known at the time, was finding God's promises about as easy to swallow as a chicken bone. The promise? That his descendants would be as numerous as the stars. The problem? No son. "No problem," came God's response.

Abram looked over at his wife Sarah as she shuffled by in her gown and slippers with the aid of a walker. The chicken bone stuck for a few minutes but eventually slid down his throat.

Just as he was turning away to invite Sarah to a candlelight dinner he heard promise number two.

"Abram."

"Yes, Lord."

"All this land will be yours."

Imagine God telling you that your children will someday own Fifth Avenue, and you will understand Abram's hesitation.

"On that one, Father, I need a little help."

And a little help was given.

It's a curious scene.

Twilight. The sky is a soft blue ceiling with starry diamonds. The air is cool. The animals in the pasture are quiet. The trees are silhouettes. Abram dozes under a tree. His sleep is fitful.

It's as if God is allowing Abram's doubt to run its course. In his dreams Abram is forced to face the lunacy of it all. The voices of doubt speak convincingly.

How do I know God is with me?

What if this is all a hoax?

How do you know that is God who is speaking?

The thick and dreadful darkness of doubt. . . .

God had told Abram to take three animals, cut them in half, and arrange the halves facing each other. To us the command is mysterious. To Abram, it wasn't. He'd seen the ceremony before. He'd participated in it. He'd sealed many covenants by walking through the divided carcasses and stating, "May what has happened to these animals happen also to me if I fail to uphold my word."

That is why his heart must have skipped a beat when he saw the lights in the darkness passing between the carcasses. The soft golden glow from the coals in the fire pot and the courageous flames from the torch. What did they mean?

The invisible God had drawn near to make his immovable promise. "To your descendants I give this land."

And though God's people often forgot their God, God didn't forget them. He kept his word. The land became theirs.

God didn't give up. He never gives up.

(From *Six Hours One Friday*
by Max Lucado)

RESPONSE

Use these questions to share more deeply with each other.

7. Why is it sometimes difficult for us to trust God's promises?

_____

_____

_____

8. What does it mean for us that God will keep his promises?

_____

_____

_____

9. What has been your reaction when God has fulfilled his promises?

_____

_____

_____

PRAYER

Father, your Word is a record of your faithfulness to promises you've made. Encourage us to trust you even when life's circumstances make it seem impossible.

JOURNALING

Take a few moments to record your personal insights from this lesson.

How is God teaching me to trust his promises about the future?

ADDITIONAL QUESTIONS

10. How has God shown faithfulness in his promises to you?

_____

_____

_____

11. How has God's faithfulness to his promises strengthened your faith?

_____

_____

_____

12. In what ways would you encourage someone who is doubting a promise of God's?

_____

_____

_____

For more Bible passages about God's promises, see Exodus 6:6–8; Joshua 13:1–7; Psalm 91; 1 Peter 1:1–21; 2 Peter 1:3,4.

To complete the Book of Genesis during this twelve-part study, read Genesis 11:1–15:21.

LESSON FIVE

RESPONSES TO PROBLEMS

REFLECTION

Begin your study by sharing thoughts on this question.

1. Think of a time when you acted out of frustration and bitterness. If you could do it over, how would you act?

_____

_____

_____

BIBLE READING

Read Genesis 16: 1–12 from the NCV or NKJV.

NCV

¹Sarai, Abram's wife, had no children, but she had a slave girl from Egypt named Hagar. ²Sarai said to Abram, "Look, the LORD has not allowed me to have children, so have sexual relations with my slave girl. If she has a child, maybe I can have my own family through her."

Abram did what Sarai said. ³It was after he had lived ten years in Canaan that Sarai gave Hagar to her husband Abram. (Hagar was her slave girl from Egypt.)

⁴Abram had sexual relations with Hagar,

NKJV

¹Now Sarai, Abram's wife, had borne him no *children*. And she had an Egyptian maidservant whose name was Hagar. ²So Sarai said to Abram, "See now, the LORD has restrained me from bearing *children*. Please, go in to my maid; perhaps I shall obtain children by her." And Abram heeded the voice of Sarai. ³Then Sarai, Abram's wife, took Hagar her maid, the Egyptian, and gave her to her husband Abram to be his wife, after Abram had dwelt ten years in the land of Canaan. ⁴So he went in to Hagar, and she

NCV

and she became pregnant. When Hagar learned she was pregnant, she began to treat her mistress Sarai badly. ⁵Then Sarai said to Abram, "This is your fault. I gave my slave girl to you, and when she became pregnant, she began to treat me badly. Let the LORD decide who is right—you or me."

⁶But Abram said to Sarai, "You are Hagar's mistress. Do anything you want to her." Then Sarai was hard on Hagar, and Hagar ran away.

⁷The angel of the LORD found Hagar beside a spring of water in the desert, by the road to Shur. ⁸The angel said, "Hagar, Sarai's slave girl, where have you come from? Where are you going?"

Hagar answered, "I am running away from my mistress Sarai."

⁹The angel of the LORD said to her, "Go home to your mistress and obey her." ¹⁰The angel also said, "I will give you so many descendants they cannot be counted."

¹¹The angel added,

"You are now pregnant,
    and you will have a son.
You will name him Ishmael,
    because the LORD has heard your cries.
¹²Ishmael will be like a wild donkey.
    He will be against everyone,
        and everyone will be against him.
    He will attack all his brothers."

NKJV

conceived. And when she saw that she had conceived, her mistress became despised in her eyes.

⁵Then Sarai said to Abram, "My wrong *be* upon you! I gave my maid into your embrace; and when she saw that she had conceived, I became despised in her eyes. The LORD judge between you and me."

⁶So Abram said to Sarai, "Indeed your maid *is* in your hand; do to her as you please." And when Sarai dealt harshly with her, she fled from her presence.

⁷Now the Angel of the LORD found her by a spring of water in the wilderness, by the spring on the way to Shur. ⁸And He said, "Hagar, Sarai's maid, where have you come from, and where are you going?"

She said, "I am fleeing from the presence of my mistress Sarai."

⁹The Angel of the LORD said to her, "Return to your mistress, and submit yourself under her hand." ¹⁰Then the Angel of the LORD said to her, "I will multiply your descendants exceedingly, so that they shall not be counted for multitude." ¹¹And the Angel of the LORD said to her:

"Behold, you *are* with child,
    And you shall bear a son.
You shall call his name Ishmael,
    Because the LORD has heard your
        affliction.
¹²   He shall be a wild man;
    His hand *shall be* against every man,
        And every man's hand against him.
    And he shall dwell in the presence of all
        his brethren."

DISCOVERY

Explore the Bible reading by discussing these questions.

2. Sarai took her frustrations out on Hagar. In what ways might she have done that?

_____

_____

_____

3. Hagar's child, Ishmael, was the father of the Arab people. Sarai's child, Isaac, was the father of the Israeli people. What were the long-term results from Sarai's taking the situation into her own hands?

_____

_____

_____

4. In what ways did Sarai's plan for having children demonstrate a lack of faith in God's plan?

_____

_____

_____

5. Hagar responded to her problems by running away. What are some modern examples of that same response?

_____

_____

_____

6. Why did Sarai react as she did when Hagar, her servant, began to despise her?

_____

_____

_____

INSPIRATION

Here is an uplifting thought from *The Inspirational Bible.*

Black and cold, bitterness denies easy escape. The sides are slippery with resentment. A floor of muddy anger stills the feet. The stench of betrayal fills the air and stings the eyes. A cloud of self-pity blocks the view of the tiny exit above.

Step in and look at the prisoners. Victims are chained to the walls. Victims of betrayal. Victims of abuse. Victims of the government, the system, the military, the world. They lift their chains as they lift their voices and wail. Loud and long they wail.

They grumble. They're angry at others who got what they didn't.

They sulk. The world is against them. . . .

You can choose, like many, to chain yourself to your hurt.

Or you can choose, like some, to put away your hurts before they become hates. You can choose to go to the party. You have a place there. Your name is beside a plate. If you are a child of God, no one can take away your sonship.

Which is precisely what the father said to the older son. "Son, you are always with me, and all that I have is yours. . . ."

And that is precisely what the Father says to you. How does God deal with your bitter heart? He reminds you that what you have is more important than what you don't have. You still have your relationship with God. No one can take that. No one can touch it.

(From *He Still Moves Stones*
by Max Lucado)

RESPONSE

Use these questions to share more deeply with each other.

7. If you were Hagar, how would you have responded to Sarai's bitter treatment?

_____

_____

_____

8. In what ways can you identify with Sarai?

_____

_____

_____

9. How could Sarai have responded to Hagar in a more Christlike manner?

_____

_____

_____

PRAYER

Father, when we feel we haven't been treated fairly or others hurt us, help us to respond in a manner that is pleasing to you. We want to glorify you no matter what the situation.

JOURNALING

Take a few moments to record your personal insights from this lesson.

How could I respond without bitterness to a problem I'm struggling with?

ADDITIONAL QUESTIONS

10. Why is it easier to run from problems rather than face them?

_____

_____

_____

11. What would be your response to someone trying to run away from a problem?

_____

_____

_____

12. How can you depend on God to help you deal with a current situation?

_____

_____

_____

For more Bible passages about responses to problems, see Exodus 1:1–21; Proverbs 15: 1,2; 15:18; 1 Corinthians 13:4–6.

To complete the Book of Genesis during this twelve-part study, read Genesis 16:1–17:27.

ADDITIONAL THOUGHTS

LESSON SIX

TRUSTING GOD

REFLECTION

Begin your study by sharing thoughts on this question.

1. Think about a time when you heard that a seemingly impossible thing would happen. How did you react?

_____

_____

_____

BIBLE READING

Read Genesis 18:1–15 and 21:1–3 from the NCV or NKJV.

NCV

¹Later, the LORD again appeared to Abraham near the great trees of Mamre. Abraham was sitting at the entrance of his tent during the hottest part of the day. ²He looked up and saw three men standing near him. When Abraham saw them, he ran from his tent to meet them. He bowed facedown on the ground before them ³and said, "Sir, if you think well of me, please stay awhile with me, your servant. ⁴I will bring some water so all of you can wash your feet. You may rest under the tree, ⁵and I will get some

NKJV

¹Then the LORD appeared to him by the terebinth trees of Mamre, as he was sitting in the tent door in the heat of the day. ²So he lifted his eyes and looked, and behold, three men were standing by him; and when he saw *them,* he ran from the tent door to meet them, and bowed himself to the ground, ³and said, "My Lord, if I have now found favor in Your sight, do not pass on by Your servant. ⁴"Please let a little water be brought, and wash your feet, and rest yourselves under the tree. ⁵"And I will bring a

NCV

bread for you so you can regain your strength. Then you may continue your journey."

The three men said, "That is fine. Do as you said."

[6]Abraham hurried to the tent where Sarah was and said to her, "Hurry, prepare twenty quarts of fine flour, and make it into loaves of bread." [7]Then Abraham ran to his herd and took one of his best calves. He gave it to a servant, who hurried to kill it and to prepare it for food. [8]Abraham gave the three men the calf that had been cooked and milk curds and milk. While they ate, he stood under the tree near them.

[9]The men asked Abraham, "Where is your wife Sarah?"

"There, in the tent," said Abraham.

[10]Then the LORD said, "I will certainly return to you about this time a year from now. At that time your wife Sarah will have a son."

Sarah was listening at the entrance of the tent which was behind him. [11]Abraham and Sarah were very old. Since Sarah was past the age when women normally have children, [12]she laughed to herself, "My husband and I are too old to have a baby."

[13]Then the LORD said to Abraham, "Why did Sarah laugh? Why did she say, 'I am too old to have a baby'? [14]Is anything too hard for the LORD? No! I will return to you at the right time a year from now, and Sarah will have a son."

[15]Sarah was afraid, so she lied and said, "I didn't laugh."

But the LORD said, "No. You did laugh." . . .

NKJV

morsel of bread, that you may refresh your hearts. After that you may pass by, inasmuch as you have come to your servant."

They said, "Do as you have said."

[6]So Abraham hurried into the tent to Sarah and said, "Quickly, make ready three measures of fine meal; knead *it* and make cakes." [7]And Abraham ran to the herd, took a tender and good calf, gave *it* to a young man, and he hastened to prepare it. [8]So he took butter and milk and the calf which he had prepared, and set *it* before them; and he stood by them under the tree as they ate.

[9]Then they said to him, "Where *is* Sarah your wife?"

So he said, "Here, in the tent."

[10]And He said, "I will certainly return to you according to the time of life, and behold, Sarah your wife shall have a son."

(Sarah was listening in the tent door which *was* behind him.) [11]Now Abraham and Sarah were old, well advanced in age; *and* Sarah had passed the age of childbearing. [12]Therefore Sarah laughed within herself, saying, "After I have grown old, shall I have pleasure, my lord being old also?"

[13]And the LORD said to Abraham, "Why did Sarah laugh, saying, 'Shall I surely bear *a child,* since I am old?' [14]"Is anything too hard for the LORD? At the appointed time I will return to you, according to the time of life, and Sarah shall have a son."

[15]But Sarah denied *it,* saying, "I did not laugh," for she was afraid.

And He said, "No, but you did laugh!" . . .

NCV

[1]The LORD cared for Sarah as he had said and did for her what he had promised. [2]Sarah became pregnant and gave birth to a son for Abraham in his old age. Everything happened at the time God had said it would. [3]Abraham named his son Isaac, the son Sarah gave birth to.

NKJV

[1]And the LORD visited Sarah as He had said, and the LORD did for Sarah as He had spoken. [2]For Sarah conceived and bore Abraham a son in his old age, at the set time of which God had spoken to him. [3]And Abraham called the name of his son who was born to him—whom Sarah bore to him—Isaac.

DISCOVERY

Explore the Bible reading by discussing these questions.

2. Sarah laughed when she heard she would be having a son. What could have been some thoughts in her head that caused that laughter?

_____

_____

_____

3. What do we know about Sarah from this event?

_____

_____

_____

4. What do you think Abraham was thinking when the Lord said he would have a son?

_____

_____

_____

5. Why did Sarah deny she had laughed?

_____

_____

_____

6. How did God respond to Sarah's lack of faith?

_____

_____

_____

INSPIRATION

Here is an uplifting thought from _The Inspirational Bible._

Consider the case of Sarai. She is in her golden years, but God promises her a son. She gets excited. She visits the maternity shop and buys a few dresses. She plans her shower and remodels her tent . . . but no son. She eats a few birthday cakes and blows out a lot of candles . . . still no son. She goes through a decade of wall calendars . . . still no son. . . .

Finally, fourteen years later, when Abram is pushing a century of years and Sarai ninety . . . when Abram has stopped listening to Sarai's advice, and Sarai has stopped giving it . . . when the wallpaper in the nursery is faded and the baby furniture is several seasons out of date . . . when the topic of the promised child brings sighs and tears and long looks into a silent sky . . . God pays them a visit and tells them they had better select a name for their new son.

Abram and Sarai have the same response: laughter. They laugh partly because it is too good to happen and partly because it might. They laugh because they have given up hope, and hope born anew is always funny before it is real. . . .

They laugh because that is what you do when someone says he can do the impossible. They laugh a little at God, and a lot with God— for God is laughing, too. Then, with the smile still on his face, he gets busy doing what he does best—the unbelievable. . . .

He changes their faith. He changes the number of their tax deductions. He changes the way they define the word impossible.

But most of all, he changes Sarah's attitude about trusting God.

(From _The Applause of Heaven_
by Max Lucado)

RESPONSE

Use these questions to share more deeply with each other.

7. Think of a time when you lacked faith in God's plan. Why did it seem unbelievable?

_____

_____

_____

8. Describe a past experience when God fulfilled a promise to you.

_____

_____

_____

9. Why do you find it difficult to believe that nothing is too hard for God to handle?

_____

_____

_____

PRAYER

We look at your plan, Father. We know that it is all based on love, yet still we have trouble trusting that you have in mind what is best for us. Help us not to look at our circumstances, but to know your will and timing are perfect.

JOURNALING

Take a few moments to record your personal insights from this lesson.

In what area of my life do I need to trust God's plan?

ADDITIONAL QUESTIONS

10. In what ways have you learned to trust God's perfect timing?

_____

_____

_____

11. What are the benefits of trusting God and his plan?

_____

_____

_____

12. In what ways would you encourage someone who is having trouble trusting God?

_____

_____

_____

For more Bible passages about trusting God, see Joshua 21:43–45; Galatians 3:5–9; 2 Timothy 4:17–18; James 2.

To complete the Book of Genesis during this twelve-part study, read Genesis 18:1–21:34.

ADDITIONAL THOUGHTS

LESSON SEVEN

COMMITMENT THROUGH TESTING

REFLECTION

Begin your study by sharing thoughts on this question.

1. Think about the hardest thing you've had to give up. Why was it so hard?

_____

_____

_____

BIBLE READING

Read Genesis 22:1–14 from the NCV or NKJV.

NCV

¹After these things God tested Abraham's faith. God said to him, "Abraham!"

And he answered, "Here I am."

²Then God said, "Take your only son, Isaac, the son you love, and go to the land of Moriah. Kill him there and offer him as a whole burnt offering on one of the mountains I will tell you about."

³Abraham got up early in the morning and saddled his donkey. He took Isaac and two servants with him. After he cut the wood for the

NKJV

¹Now it came to pass after these things that God tested Abraham, and said to him, "Abraham!"

And he said, "Here I am."

²Then He said, "Take now your son, your only *son* Isaac, whom you love, and go to the land of Moriah, and offer him there as a burnt offering on one of the mountains of which I shall tell you."

³So Abraham rose early in the morning and saddled his donkey, and took two of his young

NCV

sacrifice, they went to the place God had told them to go. ⁴On the third day Abraham looked up and saw the place in the distance. ⁵He said to his servants, "Stay here with the donkey. My son and I will go over there and worship, and then we will come back to you."

⁶Abraham took the wood for the sacrifice and gave it to his son to carry, but he himself took the knife and the fire. So he and his son went on together.

⁷Isaac said to his father Abraham, "Father!"

Abraham answered, "Yes, my son."

Isaac said, "We have the fire and the wood, but where is the lamb we will burn as a sacrifice?"

⁸Abraham answered, "God will give us the lamb for the sacrifice, my son."

So Abraham and his son went on together ⁹and came to the place God had told him about. Abraham built an altar there. He laid the wood on it and then tied up his son Isaac and laid him on the wood on the altar. ¹⁰Then Abraham took his knife and was about to kill his son.

¹¹But the angel of the LORD called to him from heaven and said, "Abraham! Abraham!"

Abraham answered, "Yes."

¹²The angel said, "Don't kill your son or hurt him in any way. Now I can see that you trust God and that you have not kept your son, your only son, from me."

¹³Then Abraham looked up and saw a male sheep caught in a bush by its horns. So Abraham went and took the sheep and killed it. He offered it as a whole burnt offering to God, and his son was saved. ¹⁴So Abraham named that place The LORD Provides. Even today

NKJV

men with him, and Isaac his son; and he split the wood for the burnt offering, and arose and went to the place of which God had told him. ⁴Then on the third day Abraham lifted his eyes and saw the place afar off. ⁵And Abraham said to his young men, "Stay here with the donkey; the lad and I will go yonder and worship, and we will come back to you."

⁶So Abraham took the wood of the burnt offering and laid *it* on Isaac his son; and he took the fire in his hand, and a knife, and the two of them went together. ⁷But Isaac spoke to Abraham his father and said, "My father!"

And he said, "Here I am, my son."

Then he said, "Look, the fire and the wood, but where *is* the lamb for a burnt offering?"

⁸And Abraham said, "My son, God will provide for Himself the lamb for a burnt offering." So the two of them went together.

⁹Then they came to the place of which God had told him. And Abraham built an altar there and placed the wood in order; and he bound Isaac his son and laid him on the altar, upon the wood. ¹⁰And Abraham stretched out his hand and took the knife to slay his son.

¹¹But the Angel of the LORD called to him from heaven and said, "Abraham, Abraham!"

So he said, "Here I am."

¹²And He said, "Do not lay your hand on the lad, or do anything to him; for now I know that you fear God, since you have not withheld your son, your only *son*, from Me."

¹³Then Abraham lifted his eyes and looked, and there behind *him was* a ram caught in a thicket by its horns. So Abraham went and took the ram, and offered it up for a burnt offering

NCV	NKJV
people say, "On the mountain of the LORD it will be provided."	instead of his son. [14]And Abraham called the name of the place, The-LORD-Will-Provide; as it is said *to* this day, "In the Mount of the LORD it shall be provided."

DISCOVERY

Explore the Bible reading by discussing these questions.

2. God commanded Abram to sacrifice his son. How did Abram respond to God's command?

_____

_____

_____

3. How do you think Abram felt when God told him to offer Isaac as a sacrifice?

_____

_____

_____

4. What does Abram's willingness to sacrifice his son reveal about his commitment to God?

_____

_____

_____

5. Why would God ask Abram to perform such a sacrifice?

_____

_____

_____

6. What is revealed about Isaac by this event?

_____

_____

_____

INSPIRATION

Here is an uplifting thought from *The Inspirational Bible.*

Stories from the underground church in [the former Soviet Union] never fail to jolt us awake. I came across another one just this past week. A house church received one copy of Gospel by Luke, the only scripture most of these Christians had ever seen. They tore it into small sections and distributed them among the body of believers. Their plan was to memorize the portion they had been given, then on the next Lord's Day they would meet and redistribute the scriptural sections.

On Sunday these believers arrived inconspicuously in small groups throughout the day so as not to arouse the suspicion of KGB informers. By dusk they were all safely inside, windows closed and doors locked. They began by singing a hymn quietly but with deep emotion. Suddenly, the door was pushed open and in walked two soldiers with loaded automatic weapons at the ready. One shouted, "All right—everybody line up against the wall. If you wish to renounce your commitment to Jesus Christ, leave now!"

Two or three quickly left, then another. After a few more seconds, two more.

"This is your last chance. Either turn against your faith in Christ," he ordered, "or stay and suffer the consequences."

Another left. Finally, two more in embarrassed silence, their faces covered, slipped out into the night. No one else moved. Parents with small children trembling beside them looked down reassuringly. They fully expected to be gunned down or, at best, to be imprisoned.

After a few moments of complete silence, the other soldier closed the door, looked back at those who stood against the wall and said, "Keep your hands up—but this time in praise to our Lord Jesus Christ, brothers and sisters. We, too, are Christians. We were sent to another house church several weeks ago to a group of believers—"

The other soldier interrupted, ". . . but, instead, we were converted! We have learned by experience, however, that unless people are willing to die for their faith, they cannot be fully trusted."

In segments of the world where Bibles are plentiful and churches are protected, faith can run awfully shallow. Commitment can stay rather lukewarm. Eagles can learn to fly dangerously low. "What we obtain too cheap, we esteem too lightly."

(From *Living Above the Level of Mediocrity* by Charles Swindoll)

RESPONSE

Use these questions to share more deeply with each other.

7. In what ways can you identify with Abram?

_____

_____

_____

8. How has God tested your commitment to him?

_____

_____

_____

9. Think of something that has been difficult for you to willingly release to God. What made it difficult?

_____

_____

_____

PRAYER

Father, renew our commitment to you by helping us release everything to you. We long to submit ourselves to you so that we might know the holy freedom available to us only through your grace.

JOURNALING

Take a few moments to record your personal insights from this lesson.

Why am I having difficulty releasing everything to God?

ADDITIONAL QUESTIONS

10. Why does God test our commitment by asking for us to release everything to him?

_____

_____

_____

11. In what ways does God test our commitment to him?

_____

_____

_____

12. Describe the parallels you see between the ram and Christ.

_____

_____

_____

For more Bible passages about commitment, see 1 Samuel 15:22; Psalm 51:17; Matthew 16:24–27.

To complete the Book of Genesis during this twelve-part study, read Genesis 22:1–26:35.

LESSON EIGHT

REACTION TO DECEIT

REFLECTION

Begin your study by sharing thoughts on this question.

1. Think of a time when you didn't get something you thought you deserved. How did you react?

_____

_____

_____

BIBLE READING

Read Genesis 27:30–41 from the NCV or NKJV.

NCV

³⁰Isaac finished blessing Jacob. Then, just as Jacob left his father Isaac, Esau came in from hunting. ³¹He also prepared some tasty food and brought it to his father. He said, "Father, rise and eat the food that your son killed for you and then bless me."

³²Isaac asked, "Who are you?" He answered, "I am your son—your firstborn son—Esau."

³³Then Isaac trembled greatly and said, "Then who was it that hunted the animals and

NKJV

³⁰Now it happened, as soon as Isaac had finished blessing Jacob, and Jacob had scarcely gone out from the presence of Isaac his father, that Esau his brother came in from his hunting. ³¹He also had made savory food, and brought it to his father, and said to his father, "Let my father arise and eat of his son's game, that your soul may bless me."

³²And his father Isaac said to him, "Who *are* you?"

NCV

brought me food before you came? I ate it, and I blessed him, and it is too late now to take back my blessing."

³⁴When Esau heard the words of his father, he let out a loud and bitter cry. He said to his father, "Bless me—me, too, my father!"

³⁵But Isaac said, "Your brother came and tricked me. He has taken your blessing."

³⁶Esau said, "Jacob is the right name for him. He has tricked me these two times. He took away my share of everything you own, and now he has taken away my blessing." Then Esau asked, "Haven't you saved a blessing for me?"

³⁷Isaac answered, "I gave Jacob the power to be master over you, and all his brothers will be his servants. And I kept him strong with grain and new wine. There is nothing left to give you, my son."

³⁸But Esau continued, "Do you have only one blessing, Father? Bless me, too, Father!" Then Esau began to cry out loud.

³⁹Isaac said to him,

"You will live far away from the best land,
  far from the rain.
⁴⁰You will live by using your sword,
    and you will be a slave to your brother.
  But when you struggle,
    you will break free from him."

⁴¹After that Esau hated Jacob because of the blessing from Isaac. He thought to himself, "My father will soon die, and I will be sad for him. Then I will kill Jacob."

NKJV

So he said, "I *am* your son, your firstborn, Esau."

³³Then Isaac trembled exceedingly, and said, "Who? Where *is* the one who hunted game and brought *it* to me? I ate all *of it* before you came, and I have blessed him—*and* indeed he shall be blessed."

³⁴When Esau heard the words of his father, he cried with an exceedingly great and bitter cry, and said to his father, "Bless me—me also, O my father!"

³⁵But he said, "Your brother came with deceit and has taken away your blessing."

³⁶And *Esau* said, "Is he not rightly named Jacob? For he has supplanted me these two times. He took away my birthright, and now look, he has taken away my blessing!" And he said, "Have you not reserved a blessing for me?"

³⁷Then Isaac answered and said to Esau, "Indeed I have made him your master, and all his brethren I have given to him as servants; with grain and wine I have sustained him. What shall I do now for you, my son?"

³⁸And Esau said to his father, "Have you only one blessing, my father? Bless me—me also, O my father!" And Esau lifted up his voice and wept.

³⁹Then Isaac his father answered and said to him:

"Behold, your dwelling shall be of the
    fatness of the earth,
  And of the dew of heaven from above.
⁴⁰ By your sword you shall live,
  And you shall serve your brother;
  And it shall come to pass, when you

NCV

NKJV

become restless,
That you shall break his yoke from your
    neck."

⁴¹So Esau hated Jacob because of the blessing with which his father blessed him, and Esau said in his heart, "The days of mourning for my father are at hand; then I will kill my brother Jacob."

DISCOVERY

Explore the Bible reading by discussing these questions.

2. Why did Jacob deceive Isaac, his father?

_____

_____

_____

3. Esau was entitled to the blessing as eldest son. How had Jacob's deception changed Esau's future?

_____

_____

_____

4. How did Esau respond to the disappointment that he wouldn't receive the blessing?

_____

_____

_____

5. What were the consequences for Esau and Jacob for both of their actions?

_____

_____

_____

6. In what ways do Jacob's actions reveal his character?

_____

_____

_____

INSPIRATION

Here is an uplifting thought from *The Inspirational Bible.*

Anger. It's easy to define: the noise of the soul. *Anger.* The unseen irritant of the heart. *Anger.* The relentless invader of silence. . . .

The louder it gets, the more desperate we become.

When we are mistreated, our animalistic response is to go on the hunt. Instinctively, we double up our fists. Getting even is natural. Which, incidentally, is precisely the problem. Revenge is natural, not spiritual. Getting even is the rule of the jungle. Giving grace is the rule of the kingdom.

Some of you are thinking, *Easy for you to say, Max, sitting there in your office . . . . You ought to try living with my wife.* Or, *You ought to have to cope with my past.* Or, *You ought to raise my kids. You don't know how my ex has mistreated me. You don't have any idea how hard my life has been.*

And you're right, I don't. But I have a very clear idea how miserable your future will be unless you deal with your anger.

X-ray the world of the vengeful and behold the tumor of bitterness: black, menacing, malignant. Carcinoma of the spirit. Its fatal fibers creep around the edge of the heart and ravage it. Yesterday you can't alter, but your reaction to yesterday you can. The past you cannot change, but your response to your past you can.

(From *When God Whispers Your Name* by Max Lucado)

RESPONSE

Use these questions to share more deeply with each other.

7. Why did Esau contemplate killing his brother?

_____

_____

_____

8. Think of a time when you have been treated unfairly. What suffering did it cause in your life?

_____

_____

_____

9. How have you dealt with the desire to "get even" or "pay back" someone who wronged you?

_____

_____

_____

PRAYER

Father, we know that bitterness and resentment don't belong in Christian hearts. But sometimes, like little children, we hold onto our hurts. Help us to turn them over to you, Father, for we do not want to live burdened and shackled lives.

JOURNALING

Take a few moments to record your personal insights from this lesson.

How do I deal with the pain I experience when others mistreat me?

ADDITIONAL QUESTIONS

10. How does God want us to react when someone hurts or deceives us?

_____

_____

_____

11. In what ways is our response to past hurts affecting the way we deal with other situations?

_____

_____

_____

12. How did Christ deal with those who hurt or deceived him?

_____

_____

_____

For more Bible passages about revenge and forgiveness, see Judges 15;
1 Samuel 24:8–12; 26: 1–25; Matthew 5:38–45; Luke 23:26–28; 1 Peter 3:8,9.

To complete the Book of Genesis during this twelve-part study, read
Genesis 27:1– 36:43.

LESSON NINE

JEALOUS BEHAVIOR

REFLECTION

Begin your study by sharing thoughts on this question.

1. In what ways has jealousy affected a relationship in your life?

_____

_____

_____

BIBLE READING

Read Genesis 37:3–20 from the NCV or NKJV.

NCV

³Since Joseph was born when his father Israel was old, Israel loved him more than his other sons. He made Joseph a special robe with long sleeves. ⁴When Joseph's brothers saw that their father loved him more than he loved them, they hated their brother and could not speak to him politely.

⁵One time Joseph had a dream, and when he told his brothers about it, they hated him even more. ⁶Joseph said, "Listen to the dream I had. ⁷We were in the field tying bundles of wheat together. My bundle stood up, and your

NKJV

³Now Israel loved Joseph more than all his children, because he *was* the son of his old age. Also he made him a tunic of *many* colors. ⁴But when his brothers saw that their father loved him more than all his brothers, they hated him and could not speak peaceably to him.

⁵Now Joseph had a dream, and he told *it* to his brothers; and they hated him even more. ⁶So he said to them, "Please hear this dream which I have dreamed: ⁷"There we were, binding sheaves in the field. Then behold, my sheaf arose and also stood upright; and indeed your

NCV	NKJV

NCV

bundles of wheat gathered around it and bowed down to it."

[8]His brothers said, "Do you really think you will be king over us? Do you truly think you will rule over us?" His brothers hated him even more because of his dreams and what he had said.

[9]Then Joseph had another dream, and he told his brothers about it also. He said, "Listen, I had another dream. I saw the sun, moon, and eleven stars bowing down to me."

[10]Joseph also told his father about this dream, but his father scolded him, saying, "What kind of dream is this? Do you really believe that your mother, your brothers, and I will bow down to you?" [11]Joseph's brothers were jealous of him, but his father thought about what all these things could mean.

[12]One day Joseph's brothers went to Shechem to graze their father's flocks. [13]Israel said to Joseph, "Go to Shechem where your brothers are grazing the flocks."

Joseph answered, "I will go."

[14]His father said, "Go and see if your brothers and the flocks are all right. Then come back and tell me." So Joseph's father sent him from the Valley of Hebron.

When Joseph came to Shechem, [15]a man found him wandering in the field and asked him, "What are you looking for?"

[16]Joseph answered, "I am looking for my brothers. Can you tell me where they are grazing the flocks?"

[17]The man said, "They have already gone. I heard them say they were going to Dothan." So Joseph went to look for his brothers and found them in Dothan.

NKJV

sheaves stood all around and bowed down to my sheaf."

[8]And his brothers said to him, "Shall you indeed reign over us? Or shall you indeed have dominion over us?" So they hated him even more for his dreams and for his words.

[9]Then he dreamed still another dream and told it to his brothers, and said, "Look, I have dreamed another dream. And this time, the sun, the moon, and the eleven stars bowed down to me."

[10]So he told *it* to his father and his brothers; and his father rebuked him and said to him, "What *is* this dream that you have dreamed? Shall your mother and I and your brothers indeed come to bow down to the earth before you?" [11]And his brothers envied him, but his father kept the matter *in mind.*

[12]Then his brothers went to feed their father's flock in Shechem. [13]And Israel said to Joseph, "Are not your brothers feeding *the flock* in Shechem? Come, I will send you to them."

So he said to him, "Here I am."

[14]Then he said to him, "Please go and see if it is well with your brothers and well with the flocks, and bring back word to me." So he sent him out of the Valley of Hebron, and he went to Shechem.

[15]Now a certain man found him, and there he was, wandering in the field. And the man asked him, saying, "What are you seeking?"

[16]So he said, "I am seeking my brothers. Please tell me where they are feeding *their flocks.*"

[17]And the man said, "They have departed from here, for I heard them say, 'Let us go to

NCV	NKJV
[18]Joseph's brothers saw him coming from far away. Before he reached them, they made a plan to kill him. [19]They said to each other, "Here comes that dreamer. [20]Let's kill him and throw his body into one of the wells. We can tell our father that a wild animal killed him. Then we will see what will become of his dreams."	Dothan.'" So Joseph went after his brothers and found them in Dothan. [18]Now when they saw him afar off, even before he came near them, they conspired against him to kill him. [19]Then they said to one another, "Look, this dreamer is coming! [20]"Come therefore, let us now kill him and cast him into some pit; and we shall say, 'Some wild beast has devoured him.' We shall see what will become of his dreams!"

DISCOVERY

Explore the Bible reading by discussing these questions.

2. Why were Joseph's brothers jealous of him?

_____

_____

_____

3. Would there have been any way for Joseph to lessen his brothers' aggravation?

_____

_____

_____

4. How did Joseph's family respond to his dreams of being in authority over them all?

_____

_____

_____

5. Why do you think Joseph told his brothers about his dreams?

_____

_____

_____

6. What brought Joseph's brothers to the point of plotting his death?

_____

_____

_____

INSPIRATION

Here is an uplifting thought from *The Inspirational Bible*.

Grudge is one of those words that defines itself. Its very sound betrays its meaning.

Say it slowly : "Grr-uuuud-ge."

It starts with a growl. " Grr . . . " Like a bear with bad breath coming out of hibernation or a mangy mongrel defending his bone in an alley. "Grr. . . ."

Being near a resentful person and petting a growling dog are equally enjoyable.

Don't you just love being next to people who are nursing a grudge? Isn't it a delight to listen to them sing their songs of woe? They are so optimistic! They are so full of hope. They are bubbling with life.

You know better. You know as well as I that if they are bubbling with anything, it is anger. And if they are full of anything, it is poisonous barbs of condemnation for all the people who have hurt them. Grudge bearers and angry animals are a lot alike. Both are irritable. Both are explosive. Both can be rabid. Someone needs to make a sign that can be worn around the neck of the resentful: "Beware of the Grrrrrrudge Bearer."

Add an M to the second part of the word, and you will see what grudge bearers throw. Mud. It's not enough to accuse; the other person's character must be attacked. It's insufficient to point a finger; a rifle must be aimed. Slander is slung. Names are called. Circles are drawn. Walls are built. And enemies are made. . . .

Is this the way you are coping with your hurts?

(From *The Applause of Heaven* by Max Lucado)

RESPONSE

Use these questions to share more deeply with each other.

7. Why do we experience feelings of jealousy?

_____

_____

_____

8. Think about a time when you became preoccupied with what someone else had. What changed about you during that time?

_____

_____

_____

9. In what ways can jealousy, if left unchecked, lead to more serious sins?

_____

_____

_____

PRAYER

Dear Father, forgive us when we become discontent with our gifts or possessions and become jealous of others. Keep our eyes focused on the many ways you've blessed us. Thank you, Father, for the unimaginable gifts of your love.

JOURNALING

Take a few moments to record your personal insights from this lesson.

What people or things am I jealous of?

ADDITIONAL QUESTIONS

10. When are you most likely to become jealous?

_____

_____

_____

11. In what area of your life do you need God's help in dealing with jealousy?

_____

_____

_____

12. In what ways does jealousy affect your relationship with God?

_____

_____

_____

For more Bible passages about jealousy, see Numbers 11:16–30; 1 Samuel 18: 1–30; Acts 5:2–18; 13:44–52.

To complete the Book of Genesis during this twelve-part study, read Genesis 37:1–38:30.

LESSON TEN

INTEGRITY

REFLECTION

Begin your study by sharing thoughts on this question.

1. Think of someone who's been an example of integrity to you. What were the evidences of his or her integrity?

_____

_____

_____

BIBLE READING

Read Genesis 39:2–12 from the NCV or NKJV.

NCV

²The LORD was with Joseph, and he became a successful man. He lived in the house of his master, Potiphar the Egyptian.

³Potiphar saw that the LORD was with Joseph and that the LORD made Joseph successful in everything he did. ⁴So Potiphar was very happy with Joseph and allowed him to be his personal servant. He put Joseph in charge of the house, trusting him with everything he owned. ⁵When Joseph was put in charge of the house and everything Potiphar owned, the LORD

NKJV

²The LORD was with Joseph, and he was a successful man; and he was in the house of his master the Egyptian. ³And his master saw that the LORD was with him and that the LORD made all he did to prosper in his hand. ⁴So Joseph found favor in his sight, and served him. Then he made him overseer of his house, and all that he had he put under his authority. ⁵So it was, from the time that he had made him overseer of his house and all that he had, that the LORD blessed the Egyptian's house for Joseph's sake;

NCV

blessed the people in Potiphar's house because of Joseph. And the LORD blessed everything that belonged to Potiphar, both in the house and in the field. ⁶So Potiphar left Joseph in charge of everything he owned and was not concerned about anything except the food he ate.

Now Joseph was well built and handsome. ⁷After some time the wife of Joseph's master began to desire Joseph, and one day she said to him, "Have sexual relations with me."

⁸But Joseph refused and said to her, "My master trusts me with everything in his house. He has put me in charge of everything he owns. ⁹There is no one in his house greater than I. He has not kept anything from me except you, because you are his wife. How can I do such an evil thing? It is a sin against God."

¹⁰The woman talked to Joseph every day, but he refused to have sexual relations with her or even spend time with her.

¹¹One day Joseph went into the house to do his work as usual and was the only man in the house at that time. ¹²His master's wife grabbed his coat and said to him, "Come and have sexual relations with me." But Joseph left his coat in her hand and ran out of the house.

NKJV

and the blessing of the LORD was on all that he had in the house and in the field. ⁶Thus he left all that he had in Joseph's hand, and he did not know what he had except for the bread which he ate.

Now Joseph was handsome in form and appearance.

⁷And it came to pass after these things that his master's wife cast longing eyes on Joseph, and she said, "Lie with me."

⁸But he refused and said to his master's wife, "Look, my master does not know what *is* with me in the house, and he has committed all that he has to my hand. ⁹*There is* no one greater in this house than I, nor has he kept back anything from me but you, because you *are* his wife. How then can I do this great wickedness, and sin against God?"

¹⁰So it was, as she spoke to Joseph day by day, that he did not heed her, to lie with her *or* to be with her.

¹¹But it happened about this time, when Joseph went into the house to do his work, and none of the men of the house *was* inside, ¹²that she caught him by his garment, saying, "Lie with me." But he left his garment in her hand, and fled and ran outside.

DISCOVERY

Explore the Bible reading by discussing these questions.

2. Describe the relationship between Potiphar and Joseph.

_____

_____

_____

3. Potiphar entrusted his whole estate to Joseph. What does that tell you about Joseph?

_____

_____

_____

4. What are some ways Joseph's integrity was or could have been tested?

_____

_____

_____

5. How did Joseph react to the continual requests of Potiphar's wife?

_____

_____

_____

6. Why did Joseph refuse to sleep with Potiphar's wife?

_____

_____

_____

INSPIRATION

Here is an uplifting thought from *The Inspirational Bible.*

Now for the sake of a few idealistic souls who could assume only the best and think, I can hardly wait to live like this; this is going to be fun! I want to bring you back ever so gently to reality. When you decide to live like Christ among the selfish and strong-willed, God will honor your decision, but . . . you will encounter misunderstanding and mistreatment. You will be taken advantage of. However, don't make another wrong assumption by thinking that if you are going through tough times, you are off target. Not so. Doing what is right is never a stroll through a rose garden. Jesus' plan for living may be simple, but it is not easy. . . .

No matter how painful it may be, let us trust Him to bring good from our living His way.

The Lord Jesus Christ is the model to follow—and you remember where He wound up! But think of all those who were once His enemies, now His friends. You and I would certainly be numbered among them. The force of love is absolutely unconquerable.

(From *Simple Faith*
by Charles Swindoll)

RESPONSE

Use these questions to share more deeply with each other.

7. What does this passage reveal about Joseph's character?

_____

_____

_____

8. Think of a situation you have experienced that tested your integrity. How did you deal with it?

_____

_____

_____

9. Think about a temptation you struggle with. In what ways could that temptation cause you to compromise your integrity?

_____

_____

_____

PRAYER

Father, when we confront temptation, we pray that you would give us strength. Use your power to block the path of evil. Thank you for your promise that if we do what is right, eventually truth and justice and goodness will prevail.

JOURNALING

Take a few moments to record your personal insights from this lesson.

How can I prepare for situations when my integrity will be tested?

ADDITIONAL QUESTIONS

10. When have you felt it necessary to flee from a tempting situation because you might sin against God?

_____

_____

_____

11. Describe some healthy options for responding to tempting situations.

_____

_____

_____

12. Describe a time when you have been misunderstood or mistreated because you did what was right.

_____

_____

_____

For more Bible passages about integrity, see Esther 7:1–10; Psalm 99:6,7; Proverbs 11, Daniel 1:1–21; Mark 12:13–17.

To complete the Book of Genesis during this twelve-part study, read Genesis 39:1–44:34.

ADDITIONAL THOUGHTS

LESSON ELEVEN

GOD'S PURPOSES ACCOMPLISHED

REFLECTION

Begin your study by sharing thoughts on this question.

1. Think of a time when you saw someone you hadn't seen in a long time. How did you react when you saw him or her?

_____

_____

_____

BIBLE READING

Read Genesis 45:1–15 from the NCV or NKJV.

NCV

¹Joseph could not control himself in front of his servants any longer, so he cried out, "Have everyone leave me." When only the brothers were left with Joseph, he told them who he was. ²Joseph cried so loudly that the Egyptians heard him, and the people in the king's palace heard about it. ³He said to his brothers, "I am Joseph. Is my father still alive?" But the brothers could not answer him, because they were very afraid of him.

⁴So Joseph said to them, "Come close to me."

NKJV

¹Then Joseph could not restrain himself before all those who stood by him, and he cried out, "Make everyone go out from me!" So no one stood with him while Joseph made himself known to his brothers. ²And he wept aloud, and the Egyptians and the house of Pharaoh heard *it*.

³Then Joseph said to his brothers, "I *am* Joseph; does my father still live?" But his brothers could not answer him, for they were dismayed in his presence. ⁴And Joseph said to

NCV

When the brothers came close to him, he said to them, "I am your brother Joseph, whom you sold as a slave to go to Egypt. ⁵Now don't be worried or angry with yourselves because you sold me here. God sent me here ahead of you to save people's lives. ⁶No food has grown on the land for two years now, and there will be five more years without planting or harvest. ⁷So God sent me here ahead of you to make sure you have some descendants left on earth and to keep you alive in an amazing way. ⁸So it was not you who sent me here, but God. God has made me the highest officer of the king of Egypt. I am in charge of his palace, and I am the master of all the land of Egypt.

⁹"So leave quickly and go to my father. Tell him, 'Your son Joseph says: God has made me master over all Egypt. Come down to me quickly. ¹⁰Live in the land of Goshen where you will be near me. Your children, your grandchildren, your flocks and herds, and all that you have will also be near me. ¹¹I will care for you during the next five years of hunger so that you and your family and all that you have will not starve.'

¹²"Now you can see for yourselves, and so can my brother Benjamin, that the one speaking to you is really Joseph. ¹³So tell my father about how powerful I have become in Egypt. Tell him about everything you have seen. Now hurry and bring him back to me." ¹⁴Then Joseph hugged his brother Benjamin and cried, and Benjamin cried also. ¹⁵And Joseph kissed all his brothers and cried as he hugged them. After this, his brothers talked with him.

NKJV

his brothers, "Please come near to me." So they came near. Then he said: "I am Joseph your brother, whom you sold into Egypt. ⁵But now, do not therefore be grieved or angry with yourselves because you sold me here; for God sent me before you to preserve life. ⁶For these two years the famine *has been* in the land, and *there are* still five years in which *there will be* neither plowing nor harvesting. ⁷And God sent me before you to preserve a posterity for you in the earth, and to save your lives by a great deliverance. ⁸So now *it was* not you *who* sent me here, but God; and He has made me a father to Pharaoh, and lord of all his house, and a ruler throughout all the land of Egypt.

⁹"Hurry and go up to my father, and say to him, 'Thus says your son Joseph: "God has made me lord of all Egypt; come down to me, do not tarry. ¹⁰You shall dwell in the land of Goshen, and you shall be near to me, you and your children, your children's children, your flocks and your herds, and all that you have. ¹¹There I will provide for you, lest you and your household, and all that you have, come to poverty; for *there are* still five years of famine."'

¹²"And behold, your eyes and the eyes of my brother Benjamin see that *it is* my mouth that speaks to you. ¹³So you shall tell my father of all my glory in Egypt, and of all that you have seen; and you shall hurry and bring my father down here."

¹⁴Then he fell on his brother Benjamin's neck and wept, and Benjamin wept on his neck. ¹⁵Moreover he kissed all his brothers and wept over them, and after that his brothers talked with him.

DISCOVERY

Explore the Bible reading by discussing these questions.

2. If you had been Joseph, how would you have revealed your identity to the brothers?

_____

_____

_____

3. What do you think ran through the mind of Joseph's brothers when he revealed his identity?

_____

_____

_____

4. Why was Joseph not angry with his brothers for selling him to Egypt?

_____

_____

_____

5. In what ways was Joseph's forgiveness for his brothers evident?

_____

_____

_____

6. Why did Joseph believe God had sent him to Egypt?

_____

_____

_____

INSPIRATION

Here is an uplifting thought from *The Inspirational Bible.*

The ultimate will of God can never be finally defeated. . . . Picture some children playing in a tiny mountainside stream. They divert the stream by making little dams of mud and stones, and they float their toy boats in the puddles and ponds. But the stream continues to surge down to the river and the valley. Now picture men building great dams, changing the course of rivers with lakes and locks, diverting their flow. Yet even they cannot prevent the streams from flowing into the sea.

In our lives, so many things—our sins and mistakes, the accidents of history, the sins of others against us—may divert and temporarily defeat God's plans and purposes. But even in new circumstances created by evils, ills, and accidents, God will provide other channels to carry out His ultimate will.

What is meant by the omnipotence of God? It does not mean that by sheer exhibition of power God gets His own way. This would make our freedom an illusion, and moral growth an impossibility. That God has power means He has the ability to achieve His purposes. To say God is all-powerful means that nothing can happen which will ultimately defeat Him.

With evil intention the establishment of Jesus' day took the innocent Son of God and crucified Him on a cross. Purely from a human standpoint, it was the most heinous crime in history. But six weeks later Christ's disciples were preaching about that very same death on the cross. God made man's crime His instrument to save the world.

Accidents, disasters, and moral evil create terrible pain. But to those of us who love God, who are called and who cooperate with His purpose, our suffering cannot separate us from His love, or defeat the working out of His purpose in our lives.

(From *Putting Away Childish Things*
by David A. Seamands)

RESPONSE

Use these questions to share more deeply with each other.

7. Describe a time when you have experienced God working his will through difficult circumstances.

_____

_____

_____

8. What lessons did you learn from this experience or another similar to it?

_____

_____

_____

9. In what ways can you stay positive during difficult times as you wait for God's will to be revealed?

_____

_____

_____

PRAYER

We pray, O Father, when we find ourselves in the dungeons of doubt, that you would hear our questions. Forgive us for demanding that you solve our problems the way we want them solved. Help us to relinquish control of our circumstances to you and let you work out your will.

JOURNALING

Take a few moments to record your personal insights from this lesson.

Why am I having difficulty trusting that God's purposes will be revealed in my life?

ADDITIONAL QUESTIONS

10. In what ways has God blessed you despite difficult circumstances you've endured?

_____

_____

_____

11. How can we trust God to work his will in our lives despite the circumstances?

_____

_____

_____

12. In what ways can you encourage someone who is struggling to trust that God's purposes will be revealed?

_____

_____

_____

For more Bible passages about God's will, see Numbers 9:1–23; 20: 1–13; Esther 9:1–32; Matthew 1:18–25; 26:36–46; Romans 1:16–32.

To complete the Book of Genesis during this twelve-part study, read Genesis 45:1–48:22.

ADDITIONAL THOUGHTS

LESSON TWELVE

FORGIVENESS

REFLECTION

Begin your study by sharing thoughts on this question.

1. Think of a time when you were unsure of someone's forgiveness. How did that feel?

_____

_____

_____

BIBLE READING

Read Genesis 50:15–21 from the NCV or NKJV.

NCV

¹⁵After Jacob died, Joseph's brothers said, "What if Joseph is still angry with us? We did many wrong things to him. What if he plans to pay us back?" ¹⁶So they sent a message to Joseph that said, "Your father gave this command before he died. ¹⁷He said to us, 'You have done wrong and have sinned and done evil to Joseph. Tell Joseph to forgive you, his brothers.' So now, Joseph, we beg you to forgive our wrong. We are the servants of the God of your father." When Joseph received the message, he cried.

¹⁸And his brothers went to him and bowed

NKJV

¹⁵When Joseph's brothers saw that their father was dead, they said, "Perhaps Joseph will hate us, and may actually repay us for all the evil which we did to him." ¹⁶So they sent *messengers* to Joseph, saying, "Before your father died he commanded, saying, ¹⁷'Thus you shall say to Joseph: "I beg you, please forgive the trespass of your brothers and their sin; for they did evil to you." ' Now, please, forgive the trespass of the servants of the God of your father." And Joseph wept when they spoke to him.

NCV

low before him and said, "We are your slaves."

¹⁹Then Joseph said to them, "Don't be afraid. Can I do what only God can do? ²⁰You meant to hurt me, but God turned your evil into good to save the lives of many people, which is being done. ²¹So don't be afraid. I will take care of you and your children." So Joseph comforted his brothers and spoke kind words to them.

NKJV

¹⁸Then his brothers also went and fell down before his face, and they said, "Behold, we *are* your servants."

¹⁹Joseph said to them, "Do not be afraid, for *am* I in the place of God? ²⁰But as for you, you meant evil against me; *but* God meant it for good, in order to bring it about as *it is* this day, to save many people alive. ²¹Now therefore, do not be afraid; I will provide for you and your little ones." And he comforted them and spoke kindly to them.

DISCOVERY

Explore the Bible reading by discussing these questions.

2. Why did Joseph's brothers try to obtain his forgiveness?

_____

_____

_____

3. Why did Joseph weep when he heard his brothers asking his forgiveness?

_____

_____

_____

4. How did Joseph respond to his brother's pleading?

_____

_____

_____

5. Why did Joseph not seek revenge on his brothers?

_____

_____

_____

6. In what ways does Joseph's forgiveness parallel God's forgiveness?

_____

_____

_____

INSPIRATION

Here is an uplifting thought from *The Inspirational Bible*.

Judgment is God's job. To assume otherwise is to assume God can't do it.

Revenge is irreverent. When we strike back we are saying, "I know vengeance is yours, God, but I just didn't think you'd punish enough. I thought I'd better take this situation into my own hands. You have a tendency to be a little soft."

Joseph understands that. Rather than get even, he reveals his identity and has his father and the rest of the family brought to Egypt. He grants them safety and provides them a place to live. They live in harmony for seventeen years.

But then Jacob dies and the moment of truth comes. The brothers have a hunch that with Jacob gone they'll be lucky to get out of Egypt with their heads on their shoulders. So they go to Joseph and plead for mercy.

"Your father gave this command before he died. . . . 'Tell Joseph to forgive you' " (Gen. 50:16,17). (I have to smile at the thought of grown men talking like this. Don't they sound like kids, whining, "Daddy said to be nice to us"?)

Joseph's response? "When Joseph received the message, he cried" (Gen. 50:17). *"What more do I have to do?"* his tears implore. *"I've given you a home. I've provided for your families. Why do you still mistrust my grace?"*

Please read carefully the two statements he makes to his brothers. First he asks, "Can I do what only God can do?" (v. 19).

May I restate the obvious? Revenge belongs to God! If vengeance is God's, then it is not ours. God has not asked us to settle the score or get even. Ever.

Why? The answer is found in the second part of Joseph's statement: "You meant to hurt me, but God turned your evil into good to save the lives of many people, which is being done" (v. 20).

Forgiveness comes easier with a wide-angle lens. Joseph uses one to get the whole picture. He refuses to focus on the betrayal of his brothers without also seeing the loyalty of his God.

It always helps to see the big picture. . . .

(From *When God Whispers Your Name* by Max Lucado)

RESPONSE

Use these questions to share more deeply with each other.

7. Describe a time when you have struggled to forgive.

_____

_____

_____

8. Why is it sometimes difficult to forgive?

_____

_____

_____

9. What steps can you take to move toward forgiving?

_____

_____

_____

PRAYER

We stand amazed, Father, that you would forgive us time and time again. Thank you for the immeasurable depth of your grace. Help us to extend that same forgiveness to others, despite the hurt and pain they may cause us.

JOURNALING

Take a few moments to record your personal insights from this lesson.

Where do I have a lack of forgiveness in my life?

ADDITIONAL QUESTIONS

10. Why does God ask us to forgive rather than seek revenge?

_____

_____

_____

11. How does it feel to know you've been forgiven by God even though you don't deserve it?

_____

_____

_____

12. In what ways can your example of forgiveness influence others?

_____

_____

_____

For more Bible passages about forgiveness, see Psalm 25:6–11; 106:1–48; Isaiah 1:1–20; Luke 7:36–48; 23:26–43; Acts 2:38.

To complete the Book of Genesis during this twelve-part study, read Genesis 49:1–50:26.

ADDITIONAL THOUGHTS

ADDITIONAL THOUGHTS

ADDITIONAL THOUGHTS

LEADERS' NOTES

LESSON ONE

Question 2: If you need to warm up your group with some more discussion, you might want to ask "If you were creating the world, what would you have done differently?"

Question 9: Here are some reflections from people in Scripture on what God's creation revealed to them about God. Job: God's sovereignty (Job 12:7-10). David: worthy of worship (Psalm 104:24-25). Psalmist: God's supremacy (Psalm 148:1-13). Paul: God's power (Romans 1:20).

LESSON TWO

Question 5: It might be helpful to make the comparison to a current relationship. What words describe a current relationship when there are things to hide and secrets to be kept?

Question 6: Include with this discussion why Adam's relationship with God was changed. Adam had no parents to create his conscience. He only had his innocence.

Question 9: You may want to read Romans 7:14—8:4 to observe the Apostle Paul's own struggle with sin in his life.

LESSON THREE

Question 1: This would be a good time to come into the discussion with your answer already prepared to break the ice.

Question 2: You might follow this question with a personal question such as, "Can any of you describe a time in your own life when you felt God was asking you to do something that the people around you would think was odd?"

Question 6: For a New Testament description of Noah's faith and character read Hebrews 11:7.

Question 8: If you discussed some personal examples after question number two, refer back to them here. Ask some of those who shared about the particular steps of faith that they took. Another example of a step of faith is found in the life of Abraham (Genesis 11:31—12:5).

LESSON FOUR

Question 6: Include in the discussion some other things that we think makes us right with God such as doing good works, earning our righteousness, not making mistakes, perfectionism.

Question 7: You may want to read aloud Hebrews 11:13-16. The great people of faith held on to promises from a distance. That is what we have to do when it is difficult to trust.

Question 8: It was very important to the Old Testament people of faith that God kept his promises. You may want to read these prayers that thank God for keeping his promises: Solomon (1 Kings 8:22-24); Nehemiah's people (Nehemiah 9:6-8).

LESSON FIVE

Question 5: Some other examples from Scripture of people who ran away include Jacob (Genesis 27:41-45); Absalom (2 Samuel 13:28-34); and Jonah (Jonah 1:1-3).

Question 8: You may want to mention in this discussion that while Sarai had certainly brought this trouble on herself, her feelings of loss, of being replaced, of being unnecessary are feelings that we all can relate to. They are also feelings that we sometimes bring on ourselves. Try to not let this discussion be a women's discussion only.

LESSON SIX

Question 1: Outside of the arena of faith and miracles, the impossible is often promised in the field of magicians and illusionists. If you know a simple magic trick it might be a good preamble to this question. If not, to get the conversation started you might mention the spectacular promises make by those illusionists: cars disappearing, bridges disappearing, etc.

Question 8: If you have such an experience, share yours first.

Question 9: Some proclamations of God's power and strength you might include here are 2 Chronicles 20:5-9; Jeremiah 32:17; Psalm 62:5-8.

LESSON SEVEN

Question 4: Some of Abram's thoughts at the time of this experience are revealed to us in Hebrews 11:17-19. He believed that one way or another God would make a way. He believed God was big enough to figure all that out.

Question 8: You might want to include in your discussion that God tested Job. Job's own statements are found in Job 23:10-12. Bring out the fact that how we live our lives determines how we persevere in a test. If we have lived righteously we know that God is testing us rather than disciplining us.

LESSON EIGHT

Question 6: You may want to point out that Jacob's name actually means "deceiver" or "the one who grabs." This was determined at the time of his birth, recorded in Genesis 25:24-26.

Question 9: Some additional verses that have to do with revenge are Leviticus 19:18; Romans 12:19; 2 Thessalonians 1:5-6. In discussing the desire to "get even" you will want to touch on the issue of forgiveness, but also of trusting that God will dispense punishment.

LESSON NINE

Question 2: Remember that Joseph's dad, Isaac, had been his mother's favorite son. This may have enabled Isaac to favor Joseph even though it enraged Joseph's brothers.

Question 4: Point out that when Joseph shared his dreams even his father scolded him. It was only Isaac, though, Scripture points out, that had the wisdom to ponder Joseph's dreams.

Question 5: If you need to prompt discussion, flesh out this question by asking, "Do you think Joseph was unaware of how the dream would affect his brothers? Is it possible he was that innocent in telling them?"

Question 9: A good example can be found in the capture and trial of Christ. Mark 15:9-11 reveals that even Pilate himself realized that envy or jealousy was a part of the motivation of the religious leaders in wanting Jesus hushed.

LESSON TEN

Question 1: If you have time you may want to look through the news to find examples of either integrity or a lack of it to lead into this question.

Question 4: Discuss a position in today's world that would be the equivalent of Joseph's position, a business manager, a CFO, a personal manager. Compare the kinds of tests or temptations people today face in those positions to what Joseph would have faced. Make the connection that Joseph was facing temptations common to our world.

Question 9: You might want to extend this discussion by including a discussion of the value of integrity today. Are there many jobs left where integrity is a prerequisite? How important to the general public is the integrity of leaders.

LESSON ELEVEN

Question 3: Review the way Joseph's brothers had treated him Genesis 37:3-5; 19-33.

Question 4: Discuss Joseph's explanation in Genesis 45:5-8. Point out that Joseph was able to give up punishing his brothers because he trusted the good that God had brought out of it.

Question 7: You may want to include Romans 8:28-29 in this discussion.

LESSON TWELVE

Question 4: Point out that Joseph never softened the blow of what his brothers had done. Even in his forgiveness he admitted that they meant to hurt him. His forgiveness wasn't predicated on the argument that someone "didn't mean to." His forgiveness was based on the foundational truth that God, ultimately, is in control of everything.

Question 9: You may want to extend this discussion into our motivation for forgiving. In several places Scripture draws a strong parallel between the forgiveness we extend to others and the forgiveness we receive from God as in Matthew 6:14-15 and Mark 11:25.

ADDITIONAL NOTES

ADDITIONAL NOTES

ADDITIONAL NOTES

ADDITIONAL NOTES

ACKNOWLEDGMENTS

Graham, Billy. *Unto the Hills,* copyright 1986, Word, Inc., Dallas, Texas.

Lucado, Max. *He Still Moves Stones,* copyright 1993, Word, Inc., Dallas, Texas.

Lucado, Max. *In the Eye of the Storm,* copyright 1991, Word, Inc., Dallas, Texas.

Lucado, Max. *Six Hours One Friday,* copyright 1989 by Max Lucado, Questar Publishers, Multnomah Books.

Lucado, Max. *The Applause of Heaven,* copyright 1990, Word, Inc., Dallas, Texas.

Lucado, Max. *When God Whispers Your Name,* copyright 1994, Word, Inc., Dallas, Texas.

Seamands, David. *Putting Away Childish Things,* Victor Books, copyright 1982, Wheaton, Illinois.

Swindoll, Charles. *Living Above the Level of Mediocrity,* copyright 1987, Word, Inc., Dallas, Texas.

Swindoll, Charles. *Simple Faith,* copyright 1991, Word Inc., Dallas, Texas.